Quiet Book Patterns

Quiet Book Patterns

25 Easy-to-Make Activities for Your Children

Amy Pincock

Plain Sight Publishing
An Imprint of Cedar Fort, Inc.
Springville, Utah

CLIPART IMAGE CREDITS:

U.S. coins courtesy of Teachers Pay Teachers (www.teacherspayteachers.com)

Princes, knight, and dragon courtesy of Cloud Street Lab (www.cloudstreetlab.com)

Road signs courtesy of Digital Scrapbooking (www.digitalscrapbooking.net)

Race car courtesy of Cloud Street Lab (www.cloudstreetlab.com)

Olympic track runners courtesy of Cloud Street Lab (www.cloudstreetlab.com)

Award medals courtesy of Teachers Pay Teachers (www.teacherspayteachers.com)

ISBN 13: 978-1-4621-1245-6

Published by Plain Sight Publishing, an imprint of Cedar Fort, Inc.
2373 W. 700 S., Springville, UT 84663
Distributed by Cedar Fort, Inc., www.cedarfort.com

Cover and page design by Angela D. Olsen
Cover design © 2013 by Lyle Mortimer
Edited by Whitney A. Lindsley

Printed in the United States of America

10 9 8 7 6 5 4 3 2

Dedicated to

My parents for helping me develop my talents
and always encouraging me.

My husband for loving and supporting me.

My children for inspiring my creative side.

Contents

Why Make a Quiet Book? 1

Getting Started. 3

Supplies 4

Finishing Your Quiet Book 5

Present

6

Circus Train

8

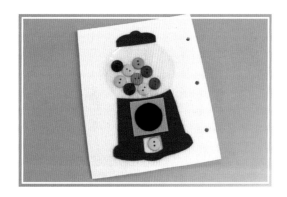

Gumball Machine

10

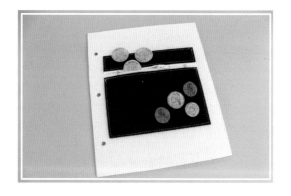

Wallet

12

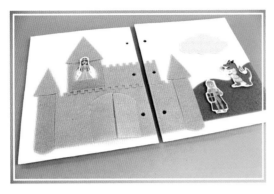

Castle Play Scene

14

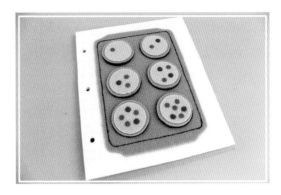

Cookie Match

16

Oven Mitt

18

Car Mat

20

Season Tree

22

Track Runners

24

Mix and Match Robot

26

Shape House

28

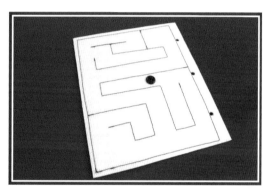

Maze

30

Art Easel

32

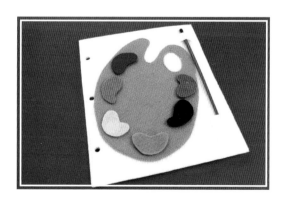

Paint Pallet

34

Chalkboard

36

Ballet Slipper

38

Noah's Ark

40

Zipper Fun

42

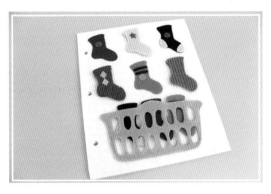

Sock Match

44

Build a House

46

Create a Face

48

Pond Scene

50

Simple Puzzles

52

Vinyl Pocket

54

Cover Page

55

Template Index. 57

Printable Images. 67

About the Author. 70

Why Make a Quiet Book?

CHILDREN LOVE TO discover how things work. Quiet books teach basic skills such as pulling a zipper, tying a bow, and buttoning a button. Children love to feel textures and manipulate objects, and quiet books are perfect for providing these experiences. Most important, they allow children to play and use their imaginations and creativity, which are what kids do best!

PLAY IS SO important. While earning my degree in family and consumer science, I studied how play contributes to healthy brain development and to the physical, social, and emotional well-being of children. Children need to run and jump and slide. They need to sing and shout and giggle. They need to put on dress-up clothes and act out real-life experiences such as playing house and school. They need to put on puppet shows and draw, paint, color, and so much more. But not all everyday events allow for these things. Sometimes we have to be quiet. Sometimes we have to wait and be still. This is when a quiet book comes in wonderfully handy.

A LOT OF homemade quiet books are difficult to put together and have unnecessary (but cute) details. I've designed my quiet book pages simply, so that even someone with the most basic sewing skills can be successful in making her book, and it won't take her years to complete it. When coming up with each page, I made sure to pick activities that would keep kids interested for a long time and give them more to discover and play with. I have given each page a lot of thought in order to provide what kids enjoy best. I hope you love making your quiet book as much as I have loved making mine.

—amy

Getting Started

CREATING A QUIET BOOK is a big project. To help things go smoother, gather all your supplies and precut all your quiet book pages out of Peltex (interfacing) before getting started. Print the page template on cardstock, cut it out, and use it as a guide. I like to place my template directly onto the Peltex and trace around it with a pencil before cutting so each page will be uniform in size.

CONSIDER THE FOLLOWING:

1. Before beginning your quiet book, plan the pages you want to make.

2. Take into consideration your child's age and skill level. Some pages are more age appropriate for toddlers, while others better match the skill level of a preschooler.

3. Be sure to read though all the instructions before beginning each quiet book page. Use the pictures as a reference for more difficult steps and as a guide as you arrange the pieces on your quiet book page.

4. Adapt each page to fit your child. For example, if you are making your quiet book for a little boy and want to make the cookie matching page, consider swapping out the pink frosting and pink sprinkles for white frosting and rainbow-colored sprinkles. Or if you are making a book for your little girl, for example, for the circus train page, make the train and clown using pink and purple felt to better appeal to her.

5. As you create each page, remember that you need a margin on the left or right side of the page to place holes for binding once your pages are complete.

THE CRAFT SUPPLY fusible web is used on most of the quiet book pages to make assembling each page simple (read more about fusible webbing in the supply section).

A FEW THINGS ABOUT FUSIBLE WEB:

IT CAN BE found under the names Pellon Wonder Under or HeatnBond.

IT IS A two-sided adhesive that glues two pieces of fabric together when heat is applied.

ONE SIDE OF the fusible web has a paper backing, and the other has adhesive. Never allow your iron to touch the other side; the adhesive will melt all over it.

BE SURE TO purchase a sewable fusible web if you will be sewing on top of it. The non-sewable kind will gum up your sewing needle.

TO USE FUSIBLE WEB WHEN MAKING YOUR QUIET BOOK:

1. Print off the quiet book template and place it underneath the fusible web with the paper side facing up. Use a pencil to trace the image onto the fusible web.

2. Bubble-cut around the shape with a pair of scissors and follow the fusible web instructions on how to iron it to your felt.

3. Once your image is applied to the felt, cut it out on the lines and remove the paper backing.

4. Place the side with the webbing down onto your quiet book page, cover it with a press cloth, and fuse it to the page using your iron.

WHEN USING FUSIBLE WEB, it's important that the images on your template are the mirror image of what you want to end up with. I've already done that work for you. The templates for each page are divided into pieces that simply need to be cut out of felt and pieces that need to be applied using the fusible web. If you choose not to use fusible web to create your quiet book pages, remember that the pieces will be backward unless you reverse the images yourself.

NOW LET'S GET STARTED!

3

Supplies

PELLON PELTEX SEW-IN—EXTRA FIRM: Peltex is a great product. I use it for my quiet book pages for a variety of reasons. Peltex makes a nice, firm base for each quiet book page and has a crisp look. It won't pill like felt and it won't fray like other fabrics. With Peltex you don't have to worry about finishing the edges or reinforcing the holes made for binding, eliminating a lot of work from your quiet book project.

FUSIBLE WEB: If you've never used this product before, you're about to find what you've been missing. fusible web allows you to eliminate 80 percent of the would-be sewing from your quiet book project. It is a paper-backed adhesive that "glues" the pieces to your quiet book page using the heat of an iron so you don't have to sew them on. I often like to top-stitch the pieces afterward to give it a more finished look, but this is not necessary. You can find fusible web under the name Pellon Wonder Under or HeatnBond.

FELT: There are all kinds of felt out there, so I won't even pretend to know about them all. My favorite kind of felt to use is the stiff felt sold in sheets at craft stores. It comes in a variety of colors and seems to hold up better than your everyday "25 cents a sheet" felt. Stiff felt won't stretch or pill and will make your quiet book look better and last longer. The cost is slightly higher with stiff felt, but with all the effort you're putting into making your quiet book, you will want it to last.

SCISSORS: A good pair of small sharp scissors is a must when making your quiet book. I use Gingher Knife Edge Sewing Scissors. Good scissors will help you cut out the small pieces with accuracy and will give your book a crisp and professional look.

TRANSFER PAPER: A few of the quiet book pages have images that you'll need to print out on transfer paper and apply to a scrap piece of Peltex. I like the Avery brand.

VELCRO: Many of the pages use Velcro. I like to use the sticky back dots unless otherwise indicated. This is another way to eliminate a lot of tedious sewing while making your book. The glue on the dots is strong and I have never had a problem with them coming off.

HOLE PUNCH: I use a single-hole paper hole punch to make the holes for binding in my quiet book pages. If you need to sharpen your hole punch, punch several holes in a piece of aluminum foil and you should be good to go.

PRESS CLOTH: A press cloth is a scrap piece of cotton fabric. Use it to cover your project when ironing on the pieces. This protects your project and your iron. Peltex and felt can melt if you place your iron directly onto them and the iron is too hot. Always use a press cloth when ironing. Better safe than sorry.

SEW-ON SNAPS: Snaps can be found in the notions section of most fabric stores. They come in many different styles and sizes. I recommend using size 4/0 of the sew-on snaps for making your quiet book.

ACID-FREE PERMANENT MARKER: A few of the quiet book pages require you to draw lines onto the page or quiet book pieces with a marker. I recommend using an acid-free permanent marker to prevent your project from yellowing over time and so the lines don't smear as you work. A fine-tip marker usually works best since the drawing required is only thin lines.

VINYL: Clear sheets of plastic vinyl are found at most fabric stores. It is usually found on a large bolt. Vinyl comes in several different gauges or thicknesses. I recommend using a medium 12 or 16 gauge.

Finishing Your Quiet Book

NOW THAT YOU'VE completed all your quiet book pages, lay them out and decide what order you want them to be in. Remember that some pages go nicely side by side like the cookie matching and oven mitt or the paint pallet and art easel.

ONCE YOU HAVE the order figured out, it's time to bind the pages.

1. Take the page template you used to cut out your Peltex pages and, with a single-hole paper hole punch, punch the holes where indicated.

2. Lay out the quiet book page that you want to be first in your book and determine if the holes will go on the right or left side of the page. Place the page template over your first quiet book page and mark where each hole will be with a pencil.

3. Using your single-hole punch, punch out the three holes. Repeat this process for the remaining pages. It's important to be accurate when doing this so the pages line up correctly. You do not need to worry about reinforcing the holes. The Peltex is strong, and the holes will not fray.

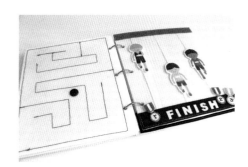

4. Once all the holes have been punched, place the first two pages back to back—lining up the holes—pin, and sew together around the page edges. Repeat for the remaining pages, taking pages two at a time, placing the them back to back, and sewing around the edges.

5. Finish off your quiet book by stringing a ribbon through each set of holes and tying a knot to keep them together or by using three 1-inch metal book rings to secure the book together.

CONGRATULATIONS on completing your quiet book! Hours of fun await one lucky child.

5

Tie a Bow on a Present

WHAT CHILDREN DO: Learning to tie their shoes can be a frustrating task for a child. This page gives kids a chance to practice in a fun, stress-free environment.

WHAT CHILDREN LEARN: Learning to tie a bow develops fine motor skills and hand-eye coordination.

What you need:

Precut Peltex page

Fusible web

Felt in various colors

Ribbon

Thread

1. Trace all shapes onto fusible web. Bubble-cut around each piece.

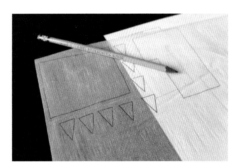

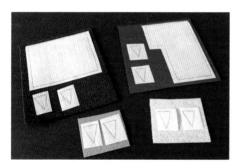

2. Follow the fusible web instructions to apply pieces to felt. Cut out each piece and remove fusible web backing.

6

3. Arrange felt pieces onto Peltex page, being sure that the side with fusible web is facing down, and then fuse them onto the page with your iron, following the fusible web instructions. If desired, top-stitch felt pieces for a more finished look.

4. Sew ribbon down the center of rectangle presents by hand or using your sewing machine. Cut a separate piece of ribbon and sew in the center at the top of present. Be sure to leave ribbon ends long

enough to make bow tying easy. (Tip: To keep ends from fraying, light a match or use a lighter and quickly run each end of the ribbon through the flame to seal.)

Circus Train with Finger Puppets

WHAT CHILDREN DO: Children can use these silly finger puppets to act out a circus scene. Puppets can be placed in the train pockets for a ride to the next circus show.

WHAT CHILDREN LEARN: These puppets make it easy to help children develop their imaginations as well as practice their storytelling skills.

What you need:

Precut Peltex page

Fusible web

Felt in various colors

Thread for sewing

1. Cut out train car pockets from felt and sew onto Peltex pages along sewing lines indicated on the template.

2. Trace remaining train pieces onto fusible web. Bubble-cut out each piece and apply to desired felt colors following fusible web instructions.

3. Cut out pieces from felt and remove backing. Piece train together using the picture as a guide. Apply to pages using your iron.

To make finger puppets:

What you need:

Fusible web

Felt in various colors

Thread for stitching puppets together

Acid-free permanent marker

Googly eyes

CLOWN Cut out two of the finger puppet forms from felt and sew together, leaving bottom open. Trace hair front and back, clown face, and mouth onto fusible web and apply to felt following fusible web instructions. Cut out and remove backing. Punch out clown nose from felt using a single-hole punch. Place hair front and back pieces together with fusible web sides touching. Sandwich sewn finger puppet in the middle. Fuse together with iron. Place face onto puppet and arrange mouth and nose on top. Fuse with iron. Glue on eyes.

8

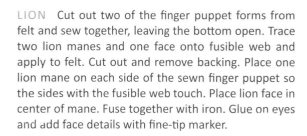

LION Cut out two of the finger puppet forms from felt and sew together, leaving the bottom open. Trace two lion manes and one face onto fusible web and apply to felt. Cut out and remove backing. Place one lion mane on each side of the sewn finger puppet so the sides with the fusible web touch. Place lion face in center of mane. Fuse together with iron. Glue on eyes and add face details with fine-tip marker.

ELEPHANT Cut out elephant back and one finger puppet form from felt. Sew together, leaving the bottom open. Trace elephant face onto fusible web and apply to felt. Cut out, remove backing and fuse to puppet front using your iron. Glue on eyes.

? What else can you do with this page?

Ask your child what his or her favorite part of the circus is. What is his or her favorite circus animal or act?

Gumball Machine

WHAT CHILDREN DO: What child doesn't love a gumball machine? Place the colorful gumballs in the opening at the top of the bowl. Insert your coin into the slot and push the gumballs out the bottom opening.

WHAT CHILDREN LEARN: This activity helps children learn color identification and sorting and helps them develop fine motor skills.

What you need:

Precut Peltex page

Fusible web

Felt in various colors

12- or 16-gauge clear vinyl

Thread for sewing

Transfer paper

Buttons or other smooth, round objects

1. Trace the gumball machine lid onto fusible web. Apply to felt following fusible web instructions. Cut out and remove backing. Place onto page and fuse together using your iron.

2. Cut out gumball bowl from vinyl. Pin to page underneath lid and sew following stitching lines indicated on template. (Tip: to keep your vinyl from sticking to your presser foot when sewing, apply a piece of matte finish scotch tape to both sides of the presser foot. This will help the vinyl slide through easily.

3. Trace circle and square pieces onto fusible web. Bubble-cut around each piece and apply to felt following fusible web instructions. Cut out pieces from felt and remove paper backing.

4. Cut out the coin pocket from felt. Pin to circle and sew together, leaving top open.

5. Cut out gumball machine base. Place square and coin circle on top and fuse together using your iron.

6. Place gumball machine base onto page slightly overlapping with vinyl bowl. Sew base to page following stitching lines indicated on the template.

7. Print out coins onto transfer paper and apply to a scrap piece of Peltex following the transfer paper instructions. Cut out coins.

8. Place buttons or other smooth, round objects into gumball machine bowl. Make sure they're small enough to come out the machine opening.

 What else can you do with this page?

Have your child count the gumballs in the machine. How many are there? Have your child sort the gumballs by color. How many red ones are there? Blue ones?

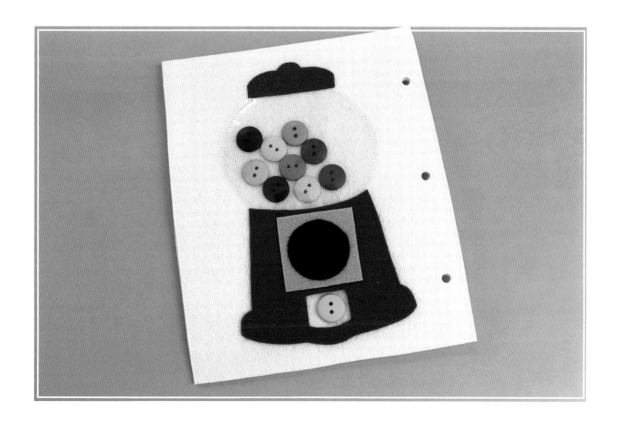

11

Wallet with Money

WHAT CHILDREN DO: This wallet has a fun zipper to open and plenty of room to store all your coins in. This page pairs well with the gumball machine page.

WHAT CHILDREN LEARN: Children can learn about each coin—their name and what they're worth. They can also practice counting and adding the coins.

What you need:

Precut Peltex page

Felt

4-inch zipper

Thread

Transfer paper

Scrap piece of Peltex

1. Cut out wallet pieces 1 and 2 from felt.

2. Pin piece 2 to the bottom side of the zipper and sew across.

3. Pin wallet onto Peltex page and sew around the three remaining sides, keeping the top side open.

4. Pin piece 1 on the top side of the zipper and sew around all four sides.

What else can you do with this page?

Help your child learn the names of each coin and how much they're worth. Ask your child: What are some good ways to earn money? Why is it important to save money?

5. Print out coins onto transfer paper and apply to a scrap piece of Peltex following the transfer paper instructions. Cut out coins.

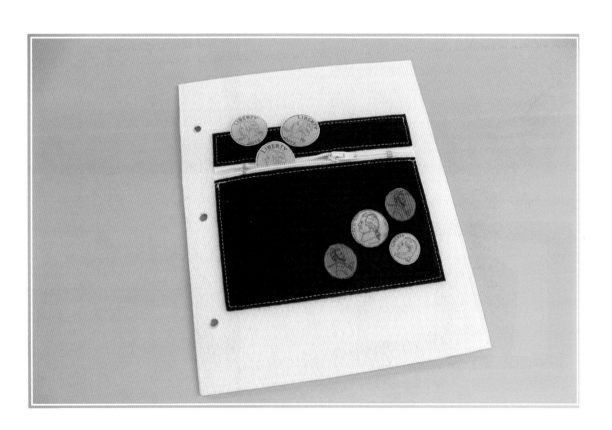

13

Castle Play Scene

WHAT CHILDREN DO: Children can create their own adventure with this castle scene. The princess and knight fit easily into a pocket behind the castle doors. The princess can also be placed in the tower window while the knight is away fighting the fearsome dragon that hides mischievously in the cloud pocket.

WHAT CHILDREN LEARN: This play scene is a fun platform for developing imagination and storytelling skills

What you need:

Precut Peltex page

Fusible web

Felt in various colors

Thread for sewing

Transfer paper

Scrap piece of Peltex

1. Cut out pocket and sew it onto Peltex page along stitching lines indicated on the template. Use template to help you place it in the correct spot where the castle door will be.

2. Trace castle pieces and grass onto fusible web. Bubble-cut around each piece. After tracing the castle onto the fusible web, cut out the spot where the castle doors will be. Apply pieces to felt following the fusible web instructions. Cut out and remove backing.

4. Lay out two Peltex pages and place castle and grass pieces onto pages (except for triangle 1). Be sure to place castle door over pocket previously sewn on. Fuse on with iron. You may need to fuse the pieces on in steps since there are so many.

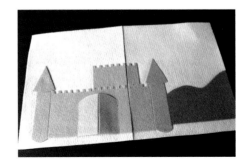

3. Take the main castle piece and cut up the center of the castle doors and across the top. Fold felt to open doors.

14

5. Cut out the castle tower with window and the cloud from felt. Sew onto page along stitching lines indicated on the template.

6. Fuse on triangle 1 above the castle tower with iron.

7. Reinforce castle door by stitching a line up both sides. Refer to template for stitching lines.

8. Print out princess, knight, and dragon onto transfer paper following the transfer paper instructions and apply to a scrap piece of Peltex. Cut out pieces.

9. Place knight and princess in pocket inside castle doors. Place dragon in cloud pocket.

What else can you do with this page?

Ask your child if dragons are pretend or real. What else is pretend? What is real?

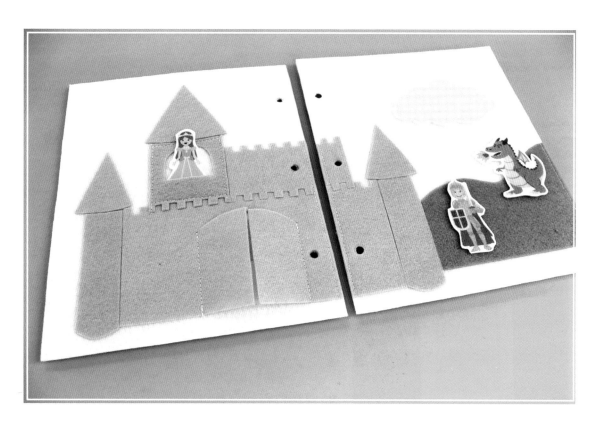

Cookie Match with Numbers & Counting

WHAT CHILDREN DO: Count the number of sprinkles on the cookies and match them to their number.

WHAT CHILDREN LEARN: Counting helps children learn numeral order. This page also teaches number recognition.

What you need:

Precut Peltex page

Fusible web

Felt in various colors

Velcro dots

Soft and flexible Velcro

Acid-free permanent marker

1. Trace the cookie sheet onto fusible web and apply to felt following the fusible web instructions. Cut out shape and remove backing.

2. Use template and marker to draw cookie sheet liner and circle outlines on felt cookie sheet.

3. Place cookie sheet onto Peltex page and fuse together using iron. Trace numbers onto fusible web. Bubble-cut around each number. Apply to back side of soft and flexible Velcro with iron. Cut out numbers and remove backing. Place numbers in circle centers on cookie sheet and apply using iron.

4. Cut out six cookies from felt.

5. Trace frosting circles onto fusible web and apply to felt. Cut out and remove backing.

6. Place frosting circles on top of cookies and fuse together with iron.

7. Apply a scrap piece of fusible web to a scrap of felt using iron. Use a single paper hole punch to punch out circle sprinkles. Remove backing.

8. Line up frosted cookies and place one sprinkle on the first cookie, two on the second, and so on, until the last cookie has six sprinkles. Fuse sprinkles on with iron.

9. Place Velcro dots on back of cookies.

What else can you do with this page?

Have your child put the cookies in order from least to greatest or greatest to least. Have them point out the even numbers and odd numbers.

17

Weave an Oven Mitt

WHAT CHILDREN DO: Create a pretty oven mitt by weaving the strips in and out. This page pairs nicely with the cookie matching page.

WHAT CHILDREN LEARN: Weaving helps to develop fine motor skills. It also teaches about patterns.

What you need:

Precut Peltex page

Fusible web

Felt in various colors

Velcro dots

Thread for sewing

1. Lay out Peltex page and lightly trace inner square of oven mitt onto page using a pencil. This will help guide you as you sew on the weaving strips.

2. Cut out weaving strips and lay them out evenly on page, three vertically, three horizontally. Sew ends onto page where indicated on template.

3. Trace oven mitt onto fusible web. Bubble-cut around shape and apply to felt. Cut out and remove backing.

4. Place oven mitt over strips, covering sewing and making sure free ends don't get caught under mitt. Apply to page using iron.

5. Add Velcro dots to free end of weaving strips.

AMY PINCOCK

Car Mat with Interchangeable Road Signs

WHAT CHILDREN DO: Children will have fun driving this sporty car all over the road, and when they're done, they can park it neatly in the garage. They also get to direct traffic by moving around the Velcro-backed road signs.

WHAT CHILDREN LEARN: The road signs teach children to understand and recognize symbols.

What you need:

Fusible web

Felt in various colors

Two precut Peltex pages

Transfer paper

Scrap piece of Peltex

Velcro

1. Trace all pieces onto fusible web (except for garage, which will be sewn on later).

2. Bubble-cut around each piece.

3. Follow the fusible web instructions and apply pieces to felt using your iron. Cut out each piece and re- move fusible web backing.

4. Lay out the two Peltex pages. Place roads on pages and fuse to pages with your iron, following the fus- ible web instructions.

5. Cut out garage piece from brown felt and sew onto Peltex page where indicated on the template.

6. Apply house pieces and garage roof to page and fuse to page with your iron. If desired, top-stitch pieces.

7. Print road signs and car on transfer paper.

8. Once printed follow the transfer paper instructions to transfer images to scrap piece of Peltex. Cut out road signs and car.

9. Place Velcro on the back of road signs and on Peltex page where you want the road signs to be.

10. Park car in the garage.

What else can you do
with this page?

Discuss with your child what each of the street signs means. Why is it important to follow the traffic rules? Where do they think the people in the car are going? Is it a long or short trip? Ask your child what activities he or she likes to do while in the car.

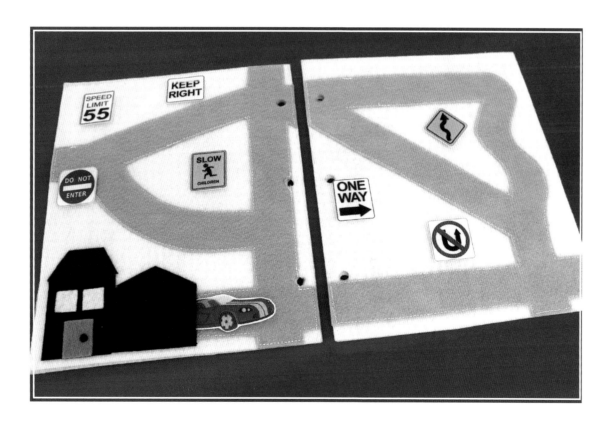

Season Tree

WHAT CHILDREN DO: Each flower and leaf snaps on to the branches of the tree. Extra pieces can be stored in the grass pocket at the bottom of the page.

WHAT CHILDREN LEARN: This little tree teaches children not only about the changing seasons but also the skill of snapping.

What you need:

Fusible web

Precut Peltex page

Felt in various colors

Snaps, size 4/0

Needle and thread

1. Trace tree trunk onto fusible web. Apply to felt following fusible web instructions. Cut out and remove backing.

2. Center tree trunk onto Peltex page and fuse together using your iron.

3. Cut out grass pocket from felt. Sew to page underneath tree trunk, leaving the top open to form a pocket.

4. Stitch five snaps onto tree branches, spaced evenly.

5. Cut out flowers, flower centers, spring leaves, and fall leaves from felt.

6. Stitch snaps onto flowers and leaves. Glue flower centers onto flowers.

7. Extra flowers and leaves can be stored in the grass pocket.

 **What else can you do with this page?**

Discuss with your child why the leaves change on trees. Why are the different seasons important?

22

Olympic Track Runners

WHAT CHILDREN DO: On your mark, get set, go! Race the runners down the track by pulling them along the ribbons. Once they reach the finish line, award them with first place, second place, and third place metals.

WHAT CHILDREN LEARN: Children learn number placement when awarding first place, second place, and third place metals.

What you need:

Precut Peltex page

Fusible web

Felt in various colors

3 pieces of ribbon, each 8 inches long

Velcro

Thread for sewing

Transfer paper

Scrap piece of Peltex

1. Print out all three track runners and award medals onto transfer paper and apply to a scrap piece of Peltex following the transfer paper instructions. Cut out pieces.

2. Use an X-Acto knife to cut two small horizontal slits the width of your ribbon about ⅛ of an inch apart from each other in the middle of each runner's shirt.

3. Starting in the back thread a ribbon up through each runner and then out the back again.

4. Space the runners evenly on the Peltex page and sew the ribbon to the page at the top and then again at the bottom.

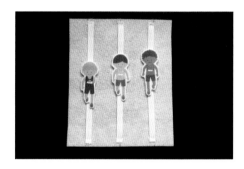

5. Trace the start line, finish line, and letters onto the fusible web and apply to felt following the fusible web instructions. Cut out.

6. Remove backing from letters and, spelling out F-I-N-I-S-H, fuse them to the finish line using your iron (do not remove the backing from finish line yet).

7. Remove backing from start and finish line and fuse to page. Be sure runners are not near iron when doing this; the heat will ruin them if touched by the iron.

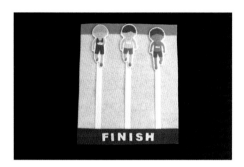

8. Cut out trophies. Apply Velcro to trophies, runners, and finish line.

What else can you do with this page?

Ask your child what the winner of the race would say to the other competitors. What does it mean to be a good sport?

Mix and Match Snap-On Robot

WHAT CHILDREN DO: The fun thing about robots is that they can be built in so many different ways. Mix and match the robot's head, arms, and legs. Extra pieces can be stored in the center body pocket.

WHAT CHILDREN LEARN: Learning to snap helps to refine fine motor skills. It also helps children gain confidence in learning to dress themselves.

What you need:

Precut Peltex page

Acid-free permanent marker

Fusible web

Felt in various colors

Snaps, size 4/0

Needle and thread

1. Cut out robot body from felt.

2. Trace robot body gadgets onto fusible web using marker. Bubble-cut around each piece and apply to individual colors of felt following fusible web instructions.

3. Cut out each piece and remove fusible web backing.

4. Place gadgets onto robot body and fuse on with your iron, following the fusible web instructions.

5. Center robot body onto Peltex page and sew on, following the lines indicated on the template, to form a pocket.

6. Cut out robot heads from felt. Trace eyes, nose, and mouths onto fusible web. Bubble-cut around each piece and apply to individual colors of felt using your iron.

7. Cut out each piece and remove fusible web backing. Punch out small circle pieces for heads 1 and 3 using a single-hole punch.

8. Place eyes, noses, and mouths onto robot heads and fuse on with your iron, following the fusible web instructions.

9. Cut out arms and legs from felt.

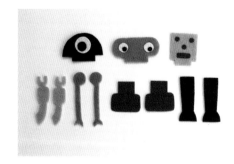

10. Use a needle and thread to sew snaps onto the Peltex page where head, arms, and legs should go, surrounding the center body pocket (five snaps total). Sew on snaps to robot heads, arms, and legs.

11. Extra robot parts can be stored in the body pocket.

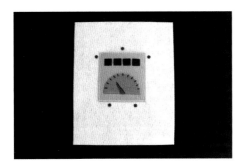

 What else can you do with this page?

Suggest your child use his or her imagination to decide what the different gadgets on the robot's body do. Get him or her thinking about the different robot parts. Ask you child if one pair of legs can run faster than another pair. Does he or she think the different heads would make different voices or speak different languages? Does one pair of arms have different skills than another?

Shape House

WHAT CHILDREN DO: Match the colored shapes to the ones on the page.

WHAT CHILDREN LEARN: This page is great for helping children to recognize shapes and colors. It also teaches children that shapes make up everyday objects around them.

What you need:

Precut Peltex page

Fusible web

Felt in various colors

Velcro dots

Acid-free permanent marker

1. Trace house, roof, and tree trunk onto fusible web. Bubble-cut around shapes and apply to felt following fusible web instructions. Cut out pieces from felt and remove backing.

2. Apply pieces to Peltex page using your iron.

3. Trace circle, triangle, square, rectangle, and oval onto page using your acid-free marker.

4. Cut out shapes in desired felt colors. Apply curtains and doorknob using fusible web.

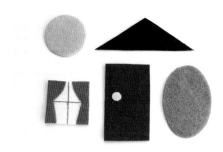

5. Apply Velcro to the page and shapes.

28

What else can you do with this page?

Help your child to name the shapes and the colors associated with them. Ask your child, "Where is the blue shape? Where does it go on the house?" Or "Can you find the oval? Where does it go?"

Maze: Two Designs to Choose From

WHAT CHILDREN DO: Push the button from one end of the maze to the other with your finger. Two designs allow you to match the skill level of your child.

WHAT CHILDREN LEARN: Mazes help children develop problem-solving skills and can improve a child's cognitive thought process.

What you need:

Precut Peltex page

Tulle

Thread for sewing

Fabric marker

Small button

1. Cut out a piece of tulle slightly larger than your Peltex page.

2. Place the tulle over the maze template and trace maze onto the tulle using a fabric marker.

3. Pin tulle firmly onto the Peltex page and sew along the maze lines drawn. Leave a small opening in the maze border and insert button. Sew up opening.

4. Trim excess tulle from around page.

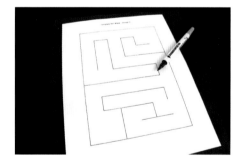

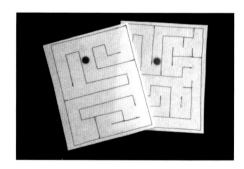

30

What else can you do with this page?

Have your children time themselves. See how fast they can get the button from one end of the maze to the other.

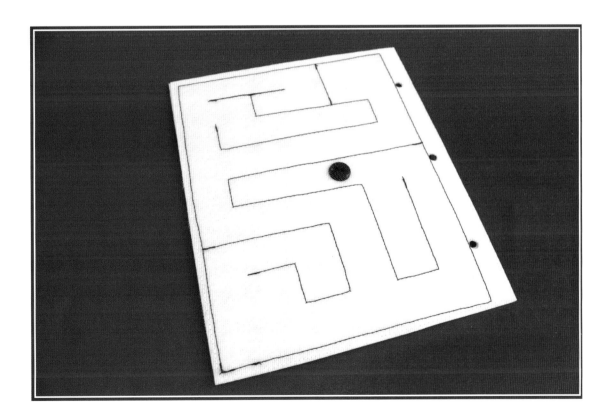

Art Easel

WHAT CHILDREN DO: Use crayons, markers, or pencils to draw a masterpiece.

WHAT CHILDREN LEARN: Drawing allows children to express their creativity, communicate visually, and polish their fine motor skills.

What you need:

Precut Peltex page

Fusible web

Felt in various colors

Thread

Cardstock

Paper

Stapler

Glue

1. Trace easel onto fusible web. Bubble-cut around shape and apply to felt following fusible web instructions. Cut out and remove backing.

2. Apply easel to Peltex page using iron.

3. Cut out easel center from felt and center it onto the easel. Sew to page, stitching along three sides, keeping top open to form a pocket.

4. Cut out cardstock and paper sheets. Stack together and secure at the top with two staples.

5. Cover staples by folding a piece of paper over the top and gluing on.

6. Insert cardstock into easel pocket.

Suggest your child write a poem or story on the notepad. If your child doesn't know how to write yet, suggest he or she draw a story using pictures and tell it to you once the picture is done. Telling stories is a great prewriting skill.

33

Paint Pallet

WHAT CHILDREN DO: Perfect for any little aspiring artist. The paint splotches Velcro onto the pallet, and the paintbrush can be used to pretend to paint everything in the quiet book.

WHAT CHILDREN LEARN: Children can learn the names of the colors. Older children can be taught about the color wheel and the results of mixing colors.

What you need:

Precut Peltex page

Fusible web

Felt in various colors

Velcro dots

Scrap piece of Peltex

Thread for sewing on pocket

Paintbrush

1. Trace paint pallet onto fusible web and iron onto felt. Cut out and remove backing. Place on Peltex page and fuse together using your iron. Top stitch around edge of paint pallet, if desired, for a more finished look.

2. Cut out paint splotches from felt.

3. Apply Velcro to paint splotches and paint pallet.

4. Cut out paintbrush pocket from Peltex and sew on page.

5. Insert paintbrush into pocket.

34

What else can you do with this page?

Have your child name the different colors on the paint pallet. Talk about what would happen if two colors got mixed together. What color would it make?

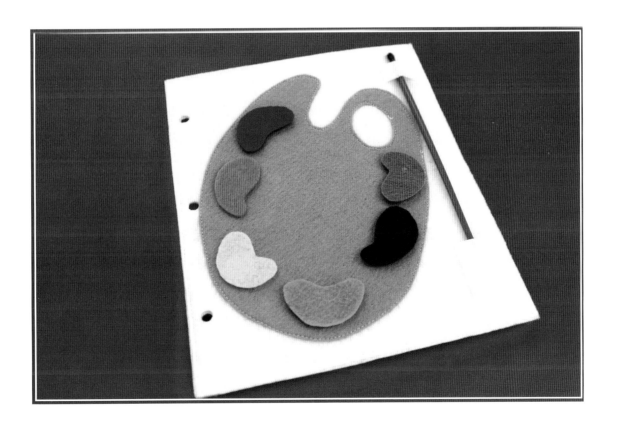

35

Chalkboard

WHAT CHILDREN DO: Drawing with chalk is fun. Children can draw whatever their heart desires and then use the flannel eraser to clean the chalkboard and draw something new.

WHAT CHILDREN LEARN: Children can polish their fine motor skills by practicing writing letters or string those letters together to make words. Drawing pictures is a great way for children to express their creativity and use their imaginations.

What you need:

Precut Peltex page

Felt in various colors

Chalkboard fabric

Thread

Chalk

Scrap piece of flannel (to use as an eraser)

1. Cut out a 5½" x 5¾" piece of chalkboard fabric.

2. Cut out frame from felt.

3. Place frame over chalkboard fabric and pin to Peltex page.

4. Stitch around on the inside and the outside of the frame.

5. Cut out pocket and sew to the bottom of the page.

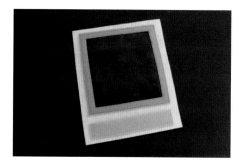

6. Place piece of chalk and flannel scrap in pocket.

What else can you do with this page?

Ask your child to write a specific letter or number for you. If the child is older ask him or her to spell a word. Suggest a scene your child can draw or have him or her draw a picture and see how quickly you can guess what it is.

Tie a Bow on a Ballet Slipper

WHAT CHILDREN DO: This sweet ballet slipper is the perfect medium for your little girl to practice learning to tie a bow.

WHAT CHILDREN LEARN: Leaning to tie a bow develops fine motor skills and hand-eye coordination.

What you need:

Precut Peltex page

Fusible web

Felt

Ribbon

Thread for sewing

1. Trace ballet slipper onto fusible web and apply to felt following fusible web instructions. Cut out slipper and remove paper backing. Place on page and fuse together using your iron.

2. Using ribbon, create a crisscross pattern coming up from the ballet slipper. Sew in place.

3. Sew a loose 20-inch piece of ribbon at the top and tie it into a bow. (Tip: To keep ends from fraying, light a match or use a lighter and quickly run each end of the ribbon through the flame to seal.)

39

Noah's Ark with Finger Puppets

WHAT CHILDREN DO: Children can use their imagination with these darling finger puppets. Have them tell you the story of Noah and the ark. Ask your child what sounds the different animals make. Where do they live? What do they eat? What is your child's favorite animal?

WHAT CHILDREN LEARN: When children tell stories, they develop oral communication and literacy skills.

What you need:

Precut Peltex page

Fusible web

Felt in various colors

Thread for stitching on ark

1. Trace the water and ark roof onto fusible web. Bubble-cut around each shape and apply to felt following the fusible web instructions. Cut out shapes and remove backing. Apply to Peltex page using iron.

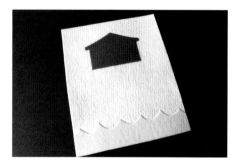

40

2. Cut out boat from felt and place on page between water and ark roof and sew onto page along stitching lines indicated on the template.

To make finger puppets:

What you need:

fusible web

Felt in various colors

Thread for stitching puppets together

Acid-free fine-tip permanent marker

Googly eyes

GIRAFFE Cut out two of the finger puppet forms from felt and sew together, leaving the bottom open. Trace two giraffe heads onto fusible web and iron onto felt. Cut out and remove backing. Cut out two giraffe knobs. Place a giraffe head on each side of the puppet form, making sure that the sides with fusible web are touching each other. Sandwich ends of giraffe knobs between ears. Fuse together with iron. Use a fine-tip marker to add nose, and glue on googly eyes.

MONKEY Cut out monkey back and one finger puppet form from felt and sew together, leaving bottom open. Trace monkey face onto fusible web and iron onto felt. Cut out and remove backing. Fuse face to puppet front. Glue on eyes and add nose and mouth with a fine-tip marker.

BEAR Cut out bear back and one finger puppet form from felt and sew together, leaving bottom open. Trace bear muzzle onto fusible web and iron onto felt. Cut out and remove backing. Fuse muzzle to puppet front. Glue on eyes and add nose with a fine-tip marker.

 What else can you do with this page?

Ask your child about the animals. Are the animals friends or enemies? What kind of adventures do they go on together while aboard the ark?

41

Zipper Fun

WHAT CHILDREN DO: Zip, zip, zip! Zippers are fun to move up and down. This simple page provides three zippers to create more entertainment.

WHAT CHILDREN LEARN: Learning to zip helps children feel confident and independent. They are so proud when they can zip their own coat!

What you need:

Precut Peltex page

3 (7-inch) zippers

Thread for sewing

1. Arrange zippers evenly onto Peltex page and pin.

2. Sew zippers onto page.

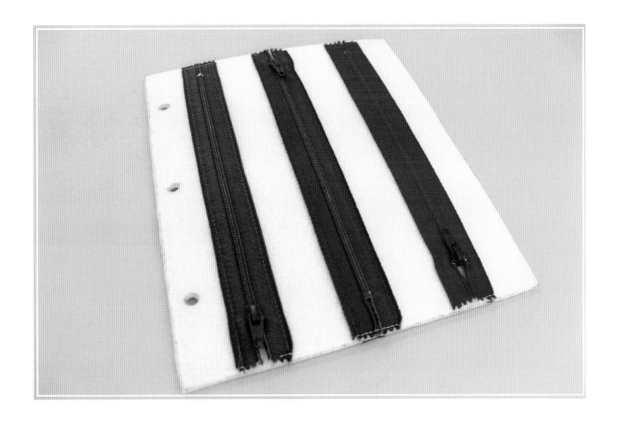

43

QUIET BOOK PATTERNS

Sock Match

WHAT CHILDREN DO: Helping Mom with laundry is fun. Match the sock to its mate to make a pair. Socks can be stored in the felt laundry basket.

WHAT CHILDREN LEARN: Matching and sorting are part of developing early math skills.

What you need:

Precut Peltex page

Fusible web

Felt in various colors

Velcro dots

Thread for sewing on laundry basket

1. Trace six socks and sock accessories onto fusible web. Bubble-cut around each piece.

2. Follow the instructions that came with your fusible web to apply pieces to individual colors of felt.

3. Cut out each piece and remove fusible web backing.

4. Arrange the socks on Peltex page. Place sock accessories on top. Apply to page using your iron.

5. Cut out the laundry basket from felt.

6. Sew laundry basket to page around edge, leaving top open to form a pocket.

7. Cut out six socks from felt. Be sure to coordinate the colors so that each sock matches one previously applied to the Peltex page.

8. Trace sock accessories onto fusible web, cut out, and apply with iron to socks.

9. Apply Velcro to all socks.

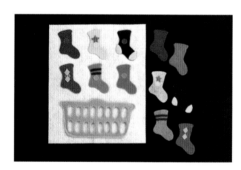

10. Sock matches can be stored in laundry basket.

44

 What else can you do
with this page?

Explain to your child what a pair is. Ask your child
what things around the house come in pairs.

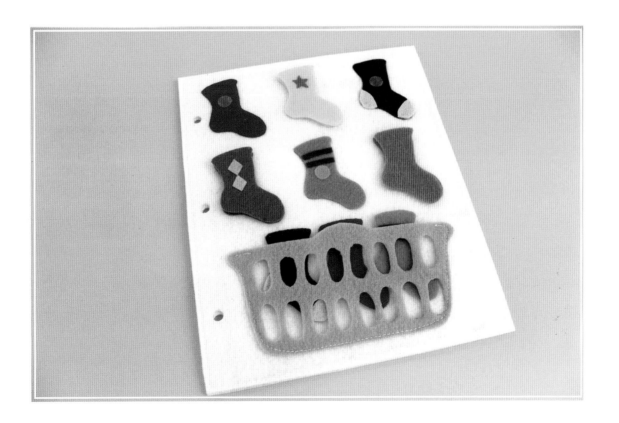

45

Build a Brick House

WHAT CHILDREN DO: This page allows children to be the builders and to create a house with a door, windows, and bricks.

WHAT CHILDREN LEARN: This activity teaches problem-solving skills as children try to fit all the pieces in the space provided.

What you need:

Precut Peltex page

Fusible web

Felt in various colors

Velcro strips

Acid-free permanent marker

1. Use an acid-free marker to draw the house shape onto the page.

2. Trace roof and chimney onto fusible web and bubble cut around each piece. Apply to felt, following the fusible web instructions.

3. Cut out and remove backing. Fuse to page using your iron.

4. Sew Velcro strips horizontally inside house, filling it up from top to bottom.

5. Cut out bricks, windows, and door from felt. Draw panes on window with marker and add a doorknob to the door by using a single-hole punch to punch out a circle from felt and gluing it to the door.

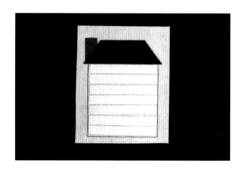

6. Apply Velcro to backs of bricks, windows, and door.

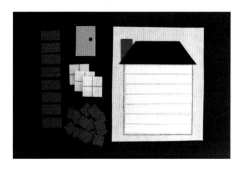

What else can you do with this page?

Discuss with your child who could live in the house. Why does a house need a door? Why does a house need a window?

Create a Face

WHAT CHILDREN DO: Use the blank head as a base to create a fun face. Make him or her sad, mysterious, happy, or silly.

WHAT CHILDREN LEARN: Children can use their imagination as they create a face, as well as learn about diversity and uniqueness.

What you need:

Precut Peltex page

Fusible web

Felt in various colors

1. Trace face shape and shirt onto fusible web. Bubble-cut out pieces and apply to felt following fusible web instructions.

2. Cut out pieces from felt and remove backing. Place on Peltex page and apply to page using your iron.

3. Choose which accessories you'd like to use for the face. Cut them out of felt. Apply any layered pieces using fusible web.

4. Store face pieces in vinyl pocket. (See page 54 for instructions on making the pocket.)

 ## What else can you do with this page?

Talk to your child about emotions. What makes your child happy? Mad? Sad? Have him or her create these emotions on the face.

48

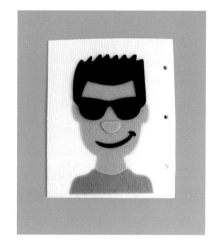

49

Pond Scene with Button-On Pictures

WHAT CHILDREN DO: Match the object to its colored button to create a beautiful outdoor scene.

WHAT CHILDREN LEARN: Buttoning develops fine motor skills. Matching is an early math skill and plays an important part in cognitive development.

What you need:

Two precut Peltex pages

Fusible web

Felt in various colors

Various colored buttons

Needle and thread

Scrap piece of Peltex

1. Trace pond, grass, and tree trunk onto fusible web. Bubble-cut around each piece and apply to individual colors of felt following fusible web instructions.

2. Cut out each piece and remove fusible web backing.

3. Lay out the two Peltex pages and place tree pieces on page. Fuse to page with your iron following the fusible web instructions.

that little fingers are going to be tugging at these buttons, so be sure to sew securely. Remove Peltex scrap and, with needle on backside, poke it through the page behind button, and pull through. Wrap thread around button several times to help secure it away from the page. Thread needle to back of page again and tie a secure knot several times.

4. Gather colored buttons and determine where each needs to be sewn. Place a scrap piece of Peltex between the page and the button to raise it slightly off the page and sew button onto page. Be careful to not sew the Peltex scrap onto the page. Little fingers will not be able to button the images on if the buttons are sewn too close to the page. Also remember

5. Cut out sun, cloud, duck, fish, bird, rabbit, and tree images out of felt, matching them to button colors. Cut slit into each piece where indicated on template with an X Acto knife.

What else can you do with this page?

Ask your child where the different animals live, what color they are, and what sounds they make. Have your child create a story with the animals as characters.

Simple Puzzles: Girl and Boy Options

WHAT CHILDREN DO: These simple shapes can be placed together to make a fun picture.

WHAT CHILDREN LEARN: Puzzles are great for developing children's hand-eye coordination and problem-solving skills.

What you need:

Precut Peltex page

Fusible web

Felt in various colors

Acid-free permanent marker

1. Cut out four puzzle bases.

2. Trace puzzle pictures onto fusible web. Bubble-cut around each shape and apply to felt following the fusible web instructions. Cut out each piece from felt and remove backing. Arrange pictures onto puzzle bases. Fuse pieces together using your iron.

3. Decide what shapes you want your puzzle pieces to be (rectangle cut into squares or long rectangles) and draw cutting lines on the back of the puzzle base with a pencil to use as a guide. Cut out.

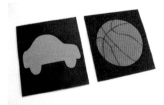

4. On your Peltex page, use the puzzle template to trace an outline of the puzzle (a rectangle with squares or long rectangles inside) using your permanent marker.

5. Store puzzle pieces in vinyl pocket. (See page 54 for instructions on making the pocket.)

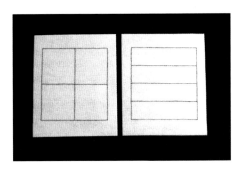

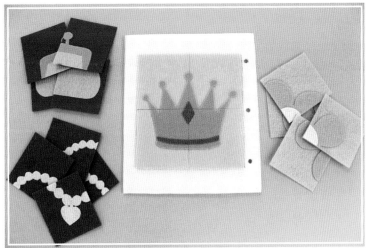

Vinyl Pocket

THIS POCKET IS perfect for accompanying many of the quiet book pages that contain a lot of small pieces. The clear front allows children to easily see what's inside. Create one or several for your book.

What you need:

Precut Peltex page

12- or 16-gauge clear vinyl

Thread for sewing

1. Cut a 7" x 7" piece of vinyl and pin it to the page.

2. Sew around three sides, leaving top open. (Tip: to keep your vinyl from sticking to your presser foot when sewing, apply a piece of matte finish Scotch tape to both sides of the presser foot. This will help the vinyl slide through easily.)

3. Fill with quiet book activity pieces.

54

Cover page

THIS PAGE MAKES a great intro to your quiet book.

What you need:

Precut Peltex page

Fusible web

Felt

1. Trace letters onto fusible web and apply to felt following the fusible web instructions.

2. Cut out letters and remove paper backing.

3. Arrange letters onto page and fuse on using your iron.

55

Template Index

Full-size templates are easily printed from the accompanying CD.

Asterisk (*) indicates that all the pieces on these pages
are reverse images to be applied using fusible web.

Present*

Circus Train 1*

Circus Train 2

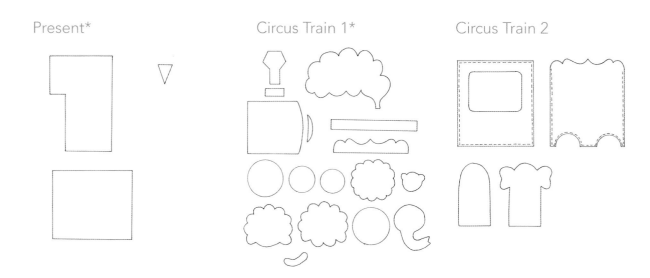

Gumball Machine 1

Gumball Machine 2*

Wallet

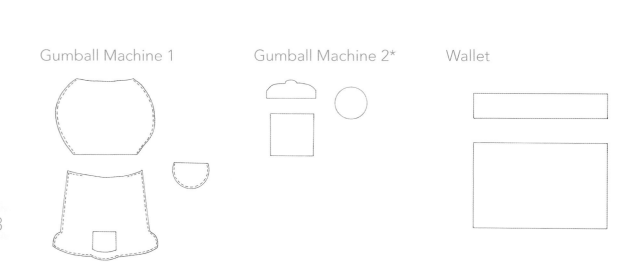

Castle Play Scene 1*

Castle Play Scene 2

Cookie Match 1*

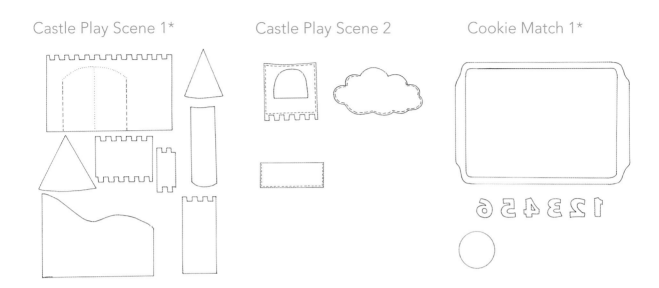

Cookie Match 2

Oven Mitt 1*

Oven Mitt 2

59

Car Mat 1*   Car Mat 2*   Car Mat 3

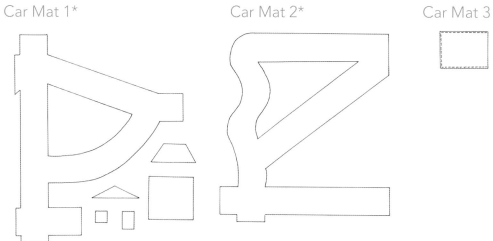

Season Tree 1*   Season Tree 2   Track Runners*

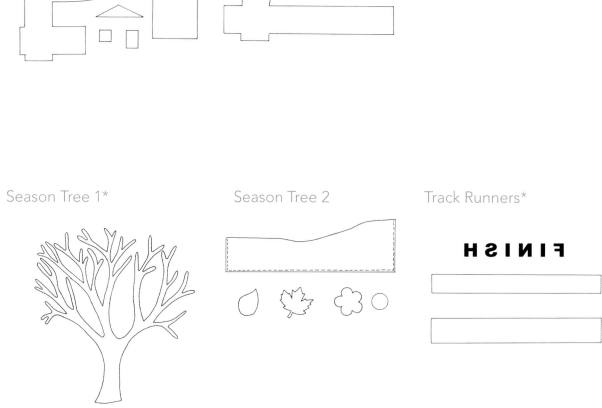

Mix and Match Robot 1

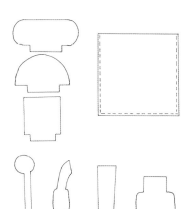

Mix and Match Robot 2*

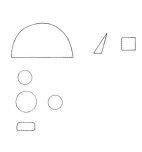

Shape House 1*

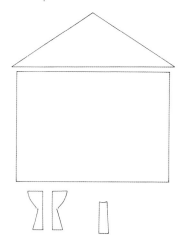

Shape House 2

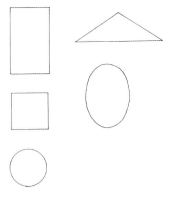

Maze 1

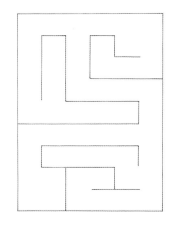

Maze 2

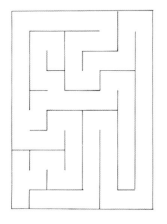

Art Easel 1

Art Easel 2

Paint Pallet 1*

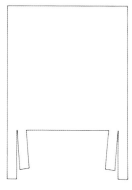

Paint Pallet 2

Chalkboard

Ballet Slipper*

Noah's Ark 1

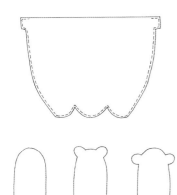

Noah's Ark 2*

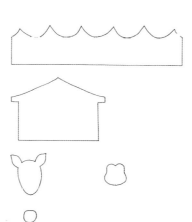

Sock Match 1

Sock Match 2*

Build a House 1

Build a House 2*

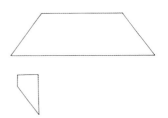

63

Create a Face 1*

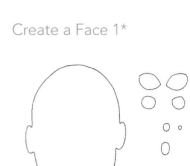

Create a Face 2

Create a Face 3

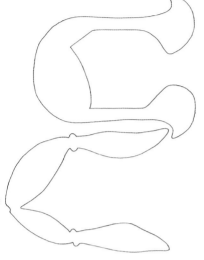

Pond Scene 1*

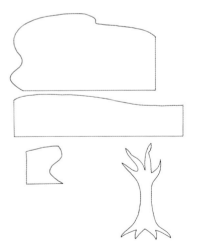

Pond Scene 2

Simple Puzzles 1

64

Simple Puzzles 2*

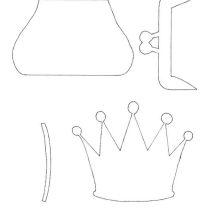

Simple Puzzles 3*

Simple Puzzles 4*

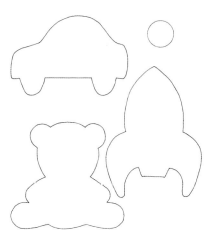

Simple Puzzles 5*

Peltex Page

Cover Page*

MY
QUIET
BOOK

65

Printable Images

Full-size templates are easily printed from the accompanying CD.

AMY PINCOCK was born into a family of crafters and sewers. As a young girl she often enjoyed stitching fabric with a needle and thread only to decide what she had made after examining her finished work. She continued to develop her skills, sewing her first dress at age ten and later earning a bachelor of science degree in family and consumer science at BYU. She now uses her creativity to educate and entertain her three children. She shares her ideas on her website WWW.SERVING-PINK-LEMONADE.COM.

0 26575 12456 9